Ridin' in the Car

Illustrated by Deborah Melmon

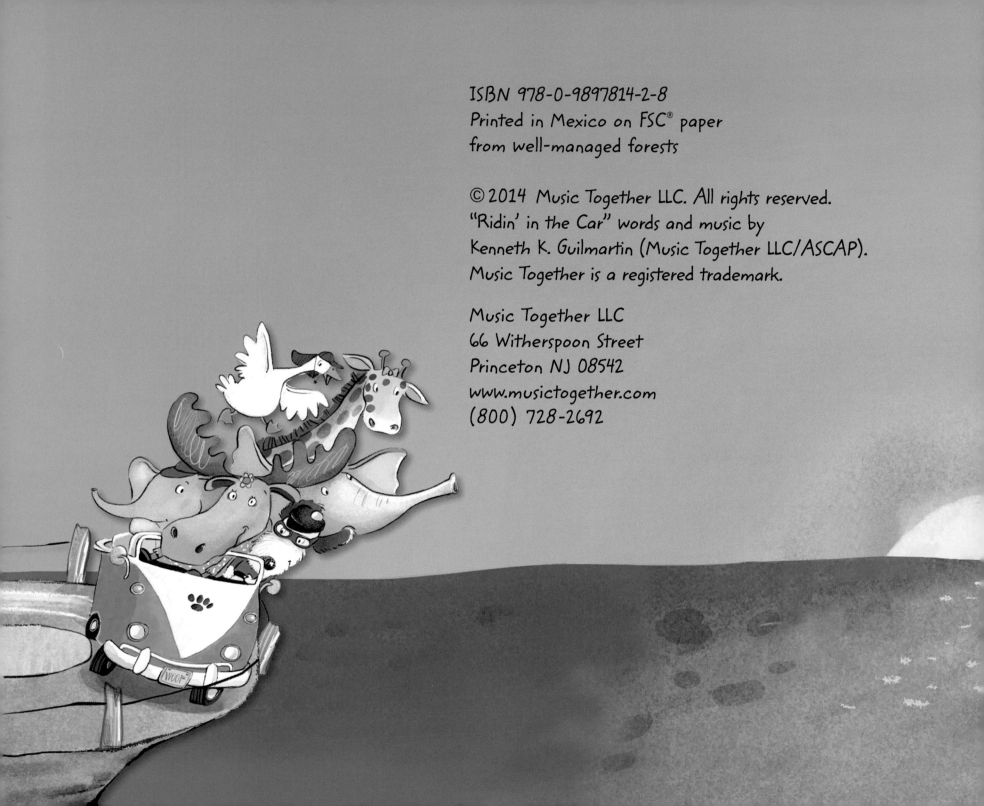

ISBN 978-0-9897814-2-8
Printed in Mexico on FSC® paper
from well-managed forests

Music Together LLC
66 Witherspoon Street
Princeton NJ 08542
www.musictogether.com
(800) 728-2692

MUSIC TOGETHER®

Ridin' in the Car

Welcome

Since 1987, Music Together has been bringing the Joy of Family Music® to young children and their families. This Singalong Storybook offers a new way to enjoy one of our best-loved Music Together songs. We invite you to sing it, read it, and use it as a starting point for conversation and imaginative play with your child.

Using the Book

If you're a Music Together family, you might start singing as soon as you turn the pages. But even if you've never attended one of our classes, you and your child can have hours of fun and learning with this Singalong Storybook. Read the story and enjoy the illustrations with your child, and then try some of the suggested activities that follow. The book can also help inspire artwork or enhance pre-literacy skills. You can even invent your own variations of the story or involve the whole family in some musical dramatic play.

Using the Recording Of course, you can also get a recording of the song to enhance your enjoyment of the book. See page 31 for ways to get the Singalong Storybook songs and see the video "Using Your Singalong Storybook Musically." Or, if you play an instrument such as piano or guitar, you'll find it easy to pick out the song using the music page at the end of the book.

Zoom, zoom, ridin' in the car,

here we go, here we go,
here we go, here we go!

Zoom, zoom, ridin' in the car,
we're goin' out today.

9

Brroom, brroom, drivin' in the car,
here we go, here we go, here we go, here we go!

Brroom, brroom, drivin' in the car,
we're goin' out today.

Brbrbr
Brbrbr
Brbrbr
Brbrbr
Brbrbr

Honk Honk
Honk

Brbrbr
Brbrbr
Brbrbr

Turn, turn, turnin' in the car,
Hold on, hold on, hold on!

Turn, turn, turnin' in the car,
you better hold on today!

Screech! Screech!
Stoppin' in the car,
watch out,
watch out,
watch out,
watch out!

Screech! Screech!
Stoppin' in the car,
you better watch out today!

Vrooom! Beep
Beep
Beep Beep
Beep

Vrooom!
Beep
Beep
Beep
Beep

19

Sing, sing, singin' in the car, la la, la la, la la, la la,

La La   La La

Sing, sing, singin' in the car,
we're singin' a song today.

21

Sleep, sleep, sleepin' in the car,

22

Mm, mm, mm, mm,

23

Sleep, sleep, sleepin' in the car, we're goin' home today.

Activities

Act It Out

Make up small movements to go along with the verses. Bounce as you "ride," turn an imaginary steering wheel as you "drive," lean to one side and then the other as you "turn," etc.

Lap Song

Your child may love taking a ride on your lap! Hold him snugly against your tummy and experiment with how bumpy or smooth a ride he'd prefer. Some children enjoy a relatively vigorous ride as long as they are cuddled safely in a loved one's arms, while others prefer a more sedate "Sunday driver" experience.

Make Up Verses

What else can you do in the car? Make up verses with your child such as "Eat, eat, eatin' in the car, Yum, yum, yum, yum . . ." or "Gas, gas, gassin' up the car, Glug, glug, glug, glug . . ."

Transportation

Invent variations for a bus, subway, tractor, train, bike, or any other mode of transportation you and your child can think of. Change the sound effects, too!

Vocal Play

Imitate the car's motor by burring your lips to make the "brrr" sound. Try singing along with the singers on the recording as they pretend to make engine and traffic noises.

Ridin' in the Car

K. Guilmartin

Brightly

1. Zoom, zoom, rid-in' in the car, here we go, here we go, here we go, here we go!
2. Brroom, broom, driv-in' in the car, here we go, here we go, here we go, here we go!

Zoom, zoom, rid-in' in the car, we're go-in' out to-day.
Brroom, broom, driv-in' in the car, we're go-in' out to-day.

3. Turn, turn, turn-in' in the car,
4. Screech! Screech! Stop-pin' in the car,
5. Sing, sing, sing-in' in the car,
(slower) 6. Sleep, sleep, sleepin' in the car,

3, 4, 5

hold on, hold on, hold on, hold on! Turn, turn, turn-in' in the car, you
watch out, watch out, watch out, watch out! Screech! Screech! Stop-pin' in the car, you
la la, la la, la la, la la, Sing, sing, sing-in' in the car, we're
mm,_____ mm,_____ mm,_____ mm,_____

6

bet-ter hold on to-day! Sleep, sleep, sleep-in in the car, we're go-in' home to-day.
bet-ter watch out to-day!
sing-in' a song to-day.

About the Song

Put on your seatbelts, we're going for a ride! In the car, children don't worry about traffic or other drivers, they simply enjoy the sheer fun of being in motion and the excitement of going someplace. This lively song, a favorite in Music Together classes, helps even adults to recapture that feeling.

WOOF

About Music Together®

Music Together classes offer a wide range of activities that are designed to be engaging and enjoyable for children from birth through age seven. By presenting a rich tonal and rhythmic mix as well as a variety of musical styles, Music Together provides children with a depth of experience that stimulates and supports their growing music skills and understanding.

Developed by Founder/Director Kenneth K. Guilmartin and his coauthor, Director of Research Lili M. Levinowitz, Ph.D., Music Together is built on the idea that all children are musical, that their parents and caregivers are a vital part of their music learning, and that their natural music abilities will flower and flourish when they are provided with a sufficiently rich learning environment.

And it's fun! Our proven methods not only help children learn to embrace and express their natural musicality—they often help their grateful grownups recapture a love of music, too. In Music Together classes all over the world, children and their families learn that music can happen anywhere, every day, at any time of the day—and they learn they can make it themselves.

Known worldwide for our mixed-age family classes, we have also adapted our curriculum to suit the needs of infants, older children, and children in school settings such as preschools, kindergartens, and early elementary grades. Visit www.musictogether.com to see video clips of Music Together classes; read about the research behind the program; purchase instruments, CDs, and books; and find a class near you. Keep singing!

Getting the Music

"Ridin' in the Car" has been sung in Music Together classes around the world. At www.musictogether.com/storybooks you can listen to the song free. You can also find it on the award-winning Music Together CD **Family Favorites**® CDs and downloads are available from Music Together, iTunes, and Amazon. To get the most out of your storybook, see the video "Using Your Singalong Storybook Musically" on our website.

The Family Favorites CD includes 19 songs and a 32-page booklet with many family activities to enjoy. Our award-winning **Family Favorites**® **Songbook for Teachers** features techniques and activities to suit a variety of classroom settings.

Come visit us at **www.musictogether.com**.

Music Together LLC

Kenneth K. Guilmartin, Founder/Director

Catherine Judd Hirsch, Director of Publishing and Marketing

Marcel Chouteau, Manager of Production and Distribution

Jill Bronson, Manager of Retail and Market Research

Susan Pujdak Hoffman, Senior Editor

Developed by Q2A/Bill Smith, New York, NY